THE BEATLES for EASY STRUMMING GUITAR

ISBN 978-1-4803-4249-1

HAL•LEONARD®
CORPORATION

7777 W. BLUEMOUND RD. P.O. BOX 13819 MILWAUKEE, WI 53213

Visit Hal Leonard Online at
www.halleonard.com

All My Loving

Words and Music by John Lennon and Paul McCartney

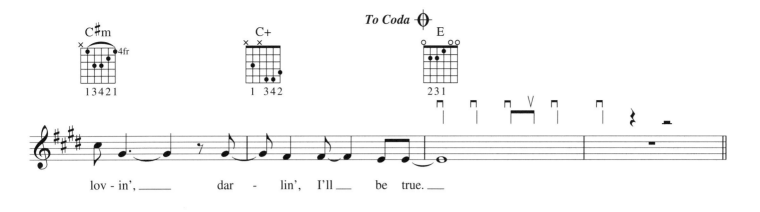

To Coda ⊕

lov - in', _____ dar - lin', I'll _____ be true. _____

Guitar Solo
w/ Chorus pattern

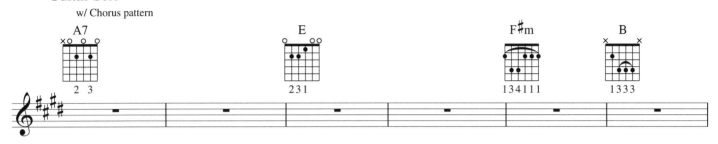

D.S. al Coda
(take 2nd ending)

⊕ **Coda**

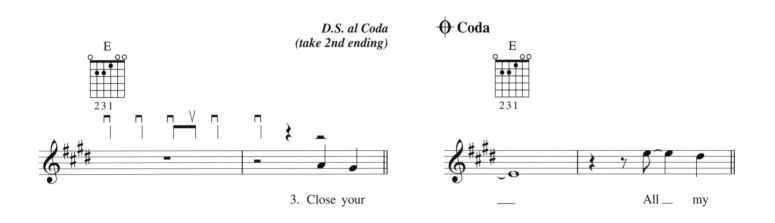

3. Close your

_____ All _____ my

Outro

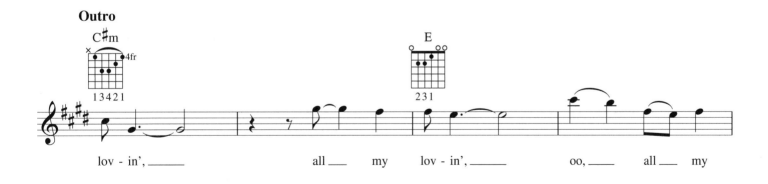

lov - in', _____ all _____ my lov - in', _____ oo, _____ all _____ my

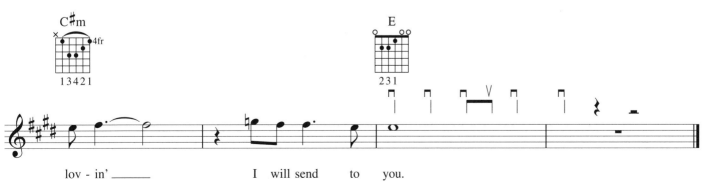

lov - in' _____ I will send to you.

And I Love Her

Words and Music by John Lennon and Paul McCartney

Intro

Moderately

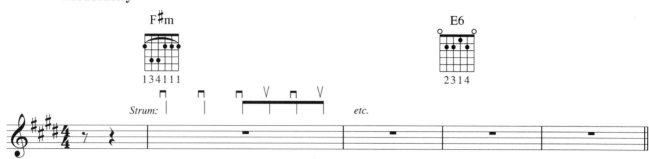

% **Verse**

1. I give her all _____ my love, __ that's all I do. __
2. She gives me ev - 'ry - thing __ and ten - der - ly. __
3. Bright are the stars _____ that shine; __ dark is the sky. __

And if you saw _____ my love, __
The kiss my lov - er brings __
I know this love _____ of mine __

To Coda ⊕

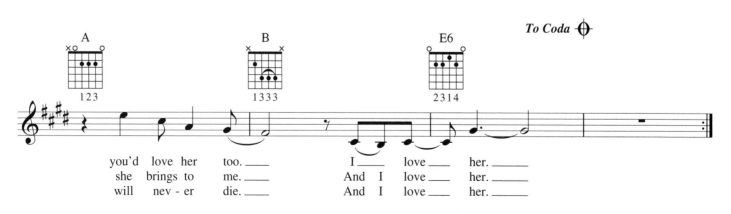

you'd love her too. _____ I love _____ her. _____
she brings to me. _____ And I love _____ her. _____
will nev - er die. _____ And I love _____ her. _____

Bridge

A love like ours ____ could nev - er die ____

D.S. al Coda

as long as I ____ have you near me. ____

Coda **Verse**

4. Bright are the stars ____ that shine; ___

dark is the sky. ____ I know this love of mine ___

will nev - er die. ____ And I love ____ her. ____

Outro

Can't Buy Me Love

Words and Music by John Lennon and Paul McCartney

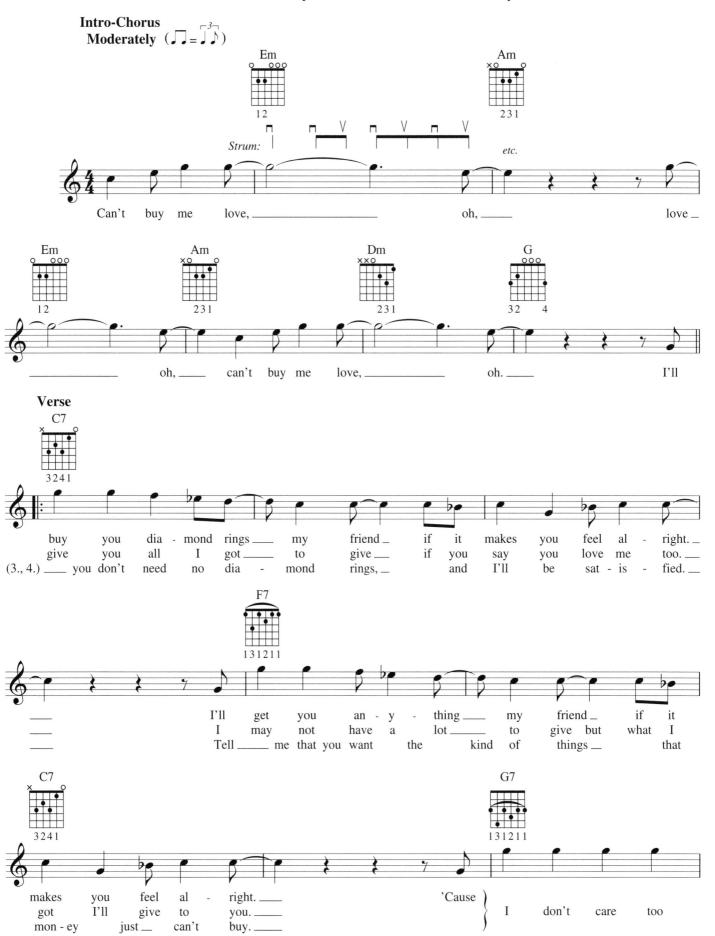

Chorus

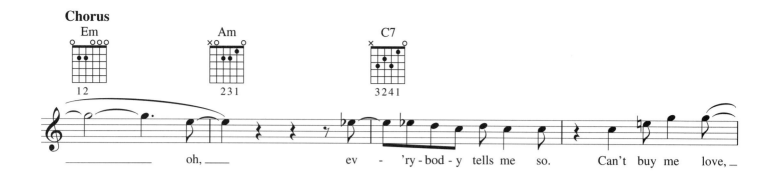

_____ oh, ____ ev - 'ry-bod - y tells me so. Can't buy me love, __

D.S. al Coda

_____ uh, no, no, no, ___ no. _____ 4. Say __

Coda

Outro-Chorus

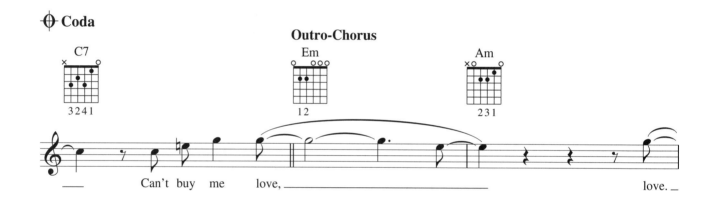

___ Can't buy me love, _____ love. _

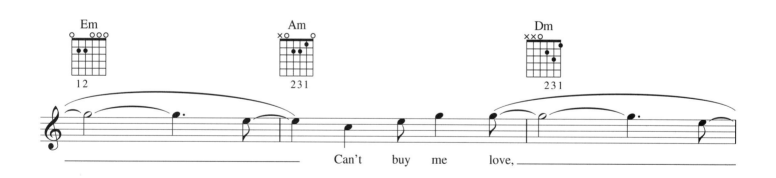

_____ Can't buy me love, _____

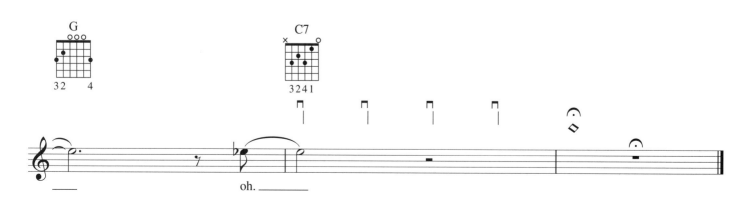

___ oh. _____

A Hard Day's Night

Words and Music by John Lennon and Paul McCartney

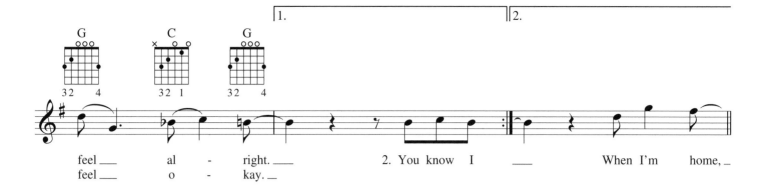

feel ___ al - right. ___   2. You know I ___ When I'm home, _
feel ___ o - kay. ___

Bridge

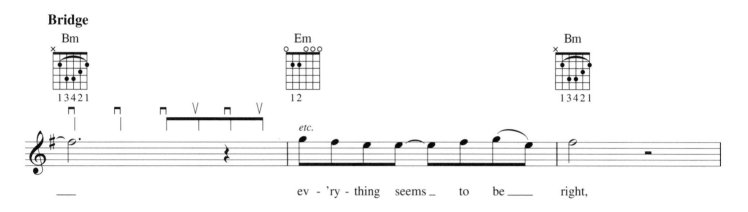

etc.

___   ev - 'ry - thing seems _ to be ___ right,

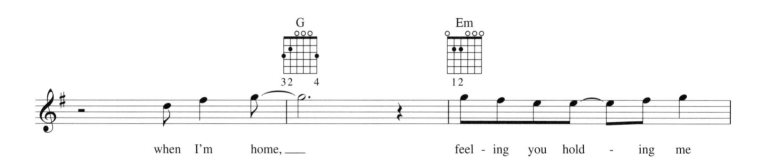

when I'm home, ___   feel - ing you hold - ing me

Verse
w/ Verse pattern

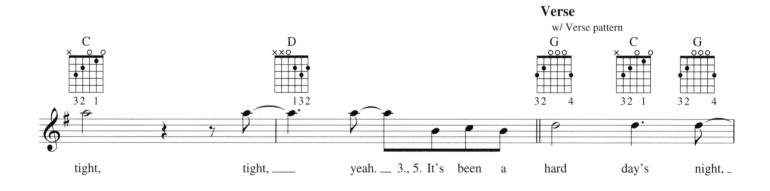

tight,   tight, ___ yeah. _ 3., 5. It's been a hard day's night, _

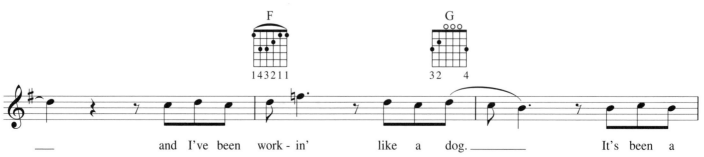

___   and I've been work - in' like a dog. ___ It's been a

hard   day's   night; ___   I should be   sleep - in'   like a   log. ___

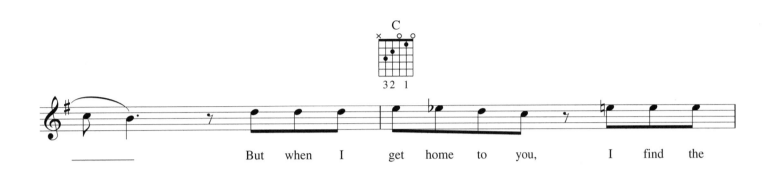

But when   I   get   home   to   you,   I   find   the

D.S. al Coda
(take 2nd ending)

To Coda ⊕

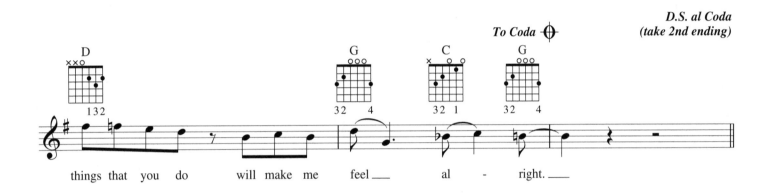

things that   you   do   will   make   me   feel ___   al   -   right. ___

⊕ **Coda**

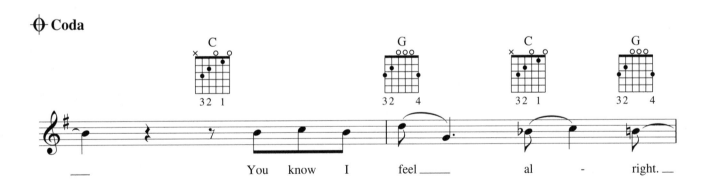

___   You   know   I   feel ___   al   -   right. ___

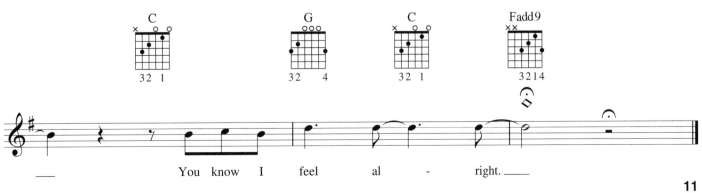

___   You   know   I   feel   al   -   right. ___

Eight Days a Week

Words and Music by John Lennon and Paul McCartney

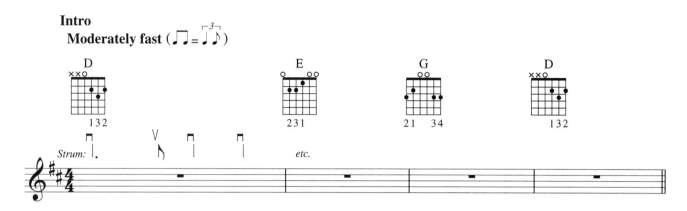

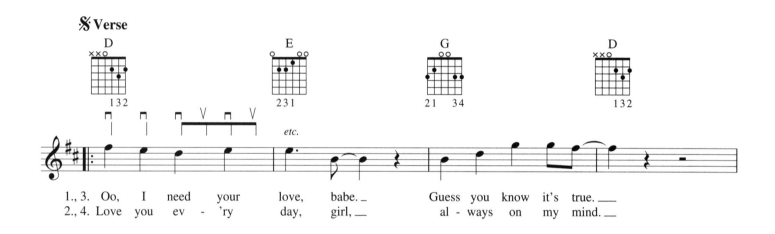

1., 3. Oo, I need your love, babe. _ Guess you know it's true. __
2., 4. Love you ev - 'ry day, girl, _ al - ways on my mind. __

Hope you need my love, babe, _ just like I need you. __
One thing I can say, girl, _ love you all the time. __

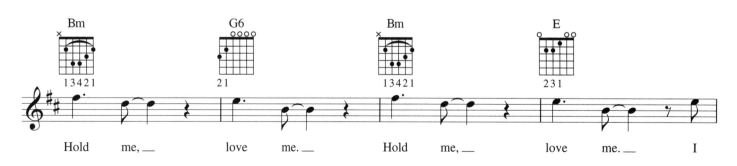

Hold me, __ love me. __ Hold me, __ love me. __ I

Hey Jude

Words and Music by John Lennon and Paul McCartney

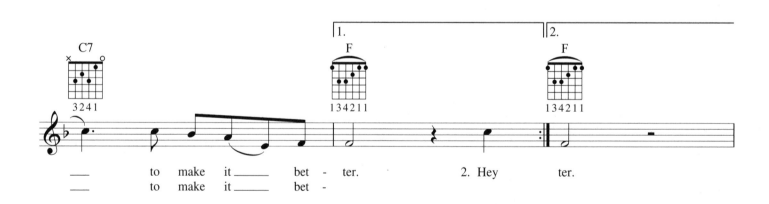

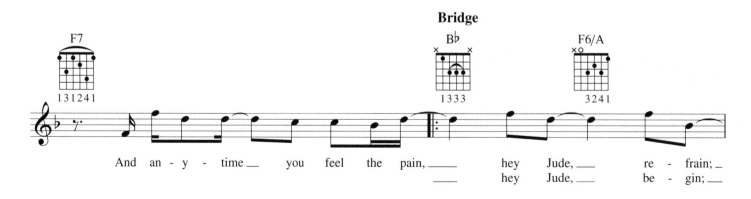

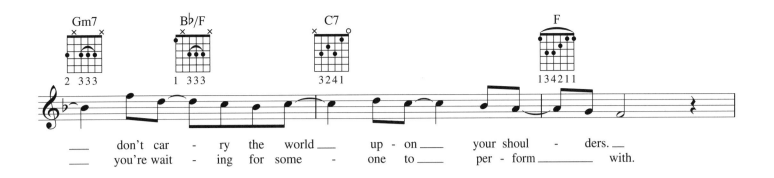

_don't car - ry the world _ up - on _ your shoul - ders. _
_you're wait - ing for some - one to _ per - form _ with.

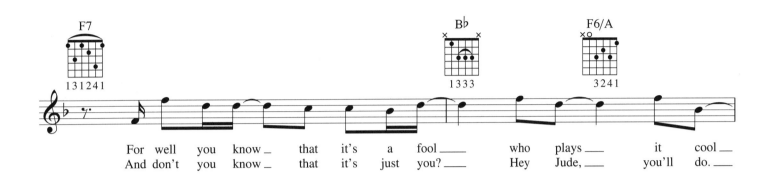

For well you know _ that it's a fool _ who plays _ it cool _
And don't you know _ that it's just you? _ Hey Jude, _ you'll do. _

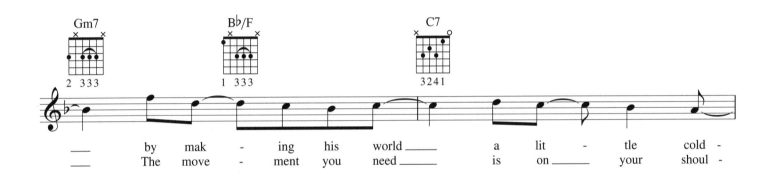

_ by mak - ing his world _ a lit - tle cold -
_ The move - ment you need _ is on _ your shoul -

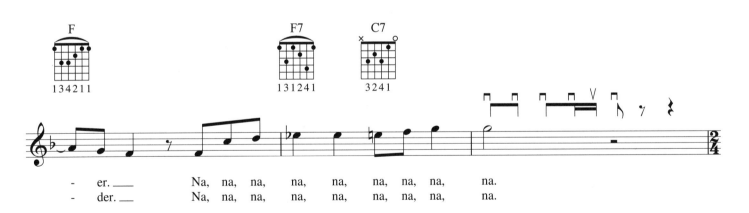

- er. _ Na, na, na, na, na, na, na, na, na.
- der. _ Na, na, na, na, na, na, na, na, na.

Verse

w/ Verse pattern

3. Hey _ Jude, don't let me down. You have
4. Hey _ Jude, don't make it bad; take a

15

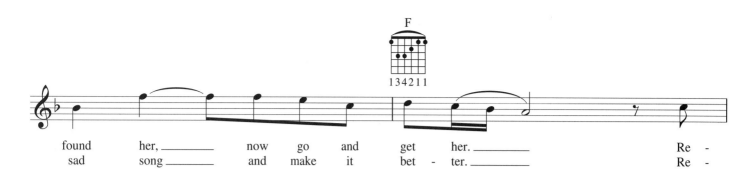

found her, _____ now go and get her. _____ Re -
sad song _____ and make it bet - ter. _____ Re -

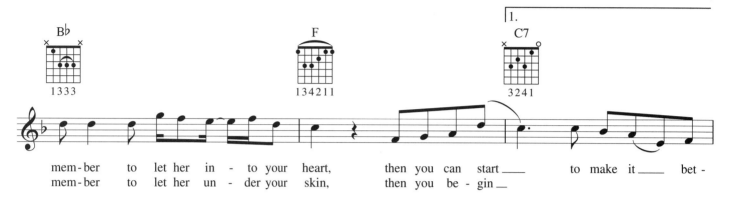

mem - ber to let her in - to your heart, then you can start _____ to make it _____ bet -
mem - ber to let her un - der your skin, then you be - gin _____

ter. So let it out _____ and let it in, _____ _____ to make it bet -

Outro
w/ Verse pattern

- ter, bet - ter, bet - ter, bet - ter, bet - ter, bet - ter, oh! Na, na, na,

Repeat and fade

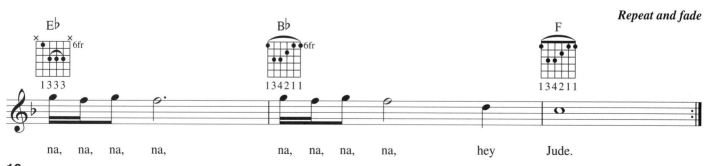

na, na, na, na, na, na, na, na, hey Jude.

I Want to Hold Your Hand

Words and Music by John Lennon and Paul McCartney

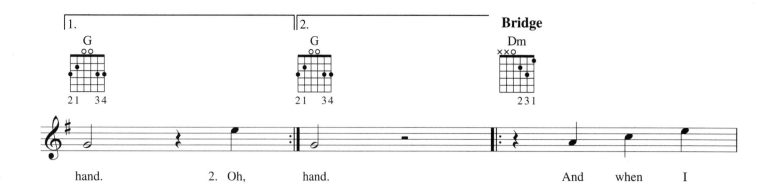

hand. 2. Oh, hand. And when I

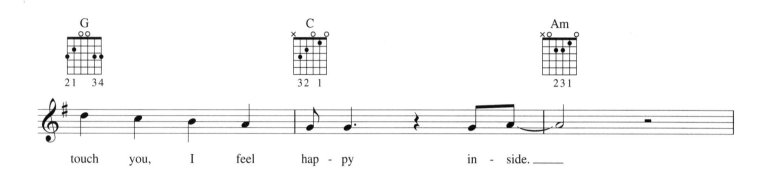

touch you, I feel hap - py in - side. _____

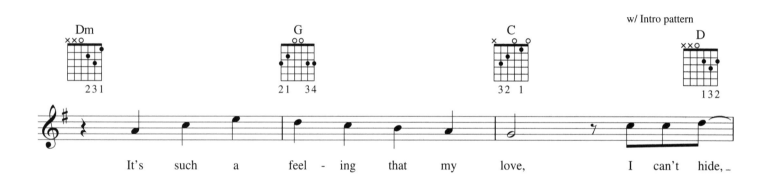

It's such a feel - ing that my love, I can't hide, _

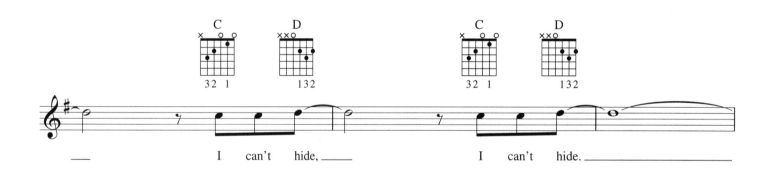

_____ I can't hide, _____ I can't hide. _____

Verse

w/ Verse pattern

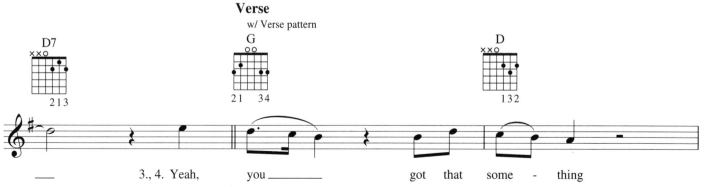

_____ 3., 4. Yeah, you _____ got that some - thing

18

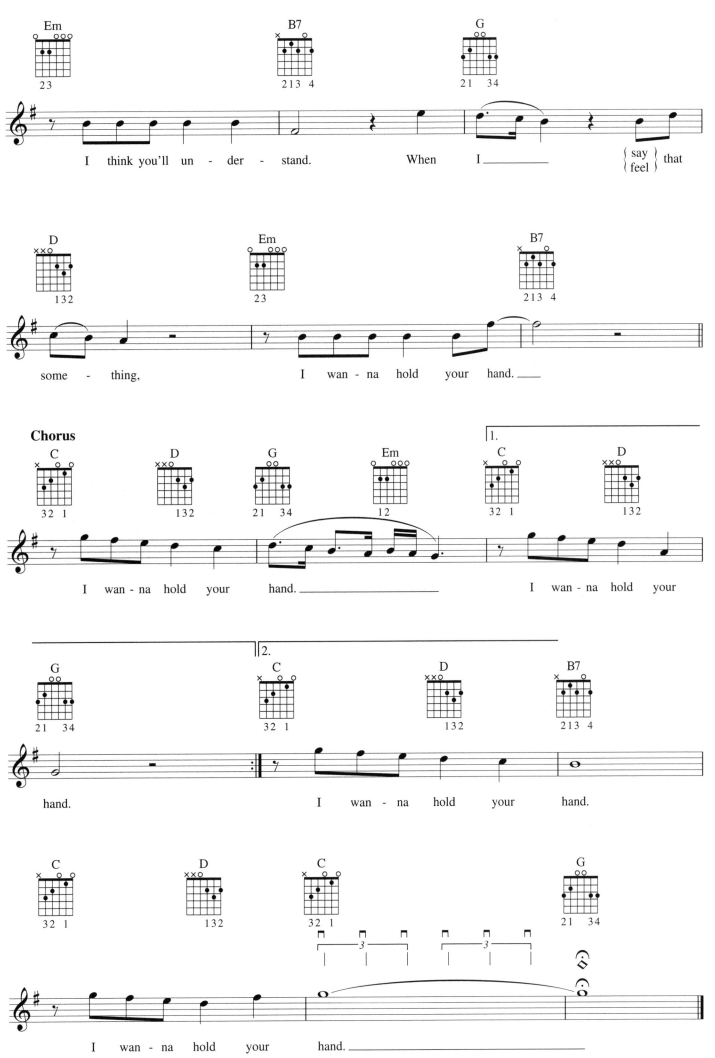

I Will

Words and Music by John Lennon and Paul McCartney

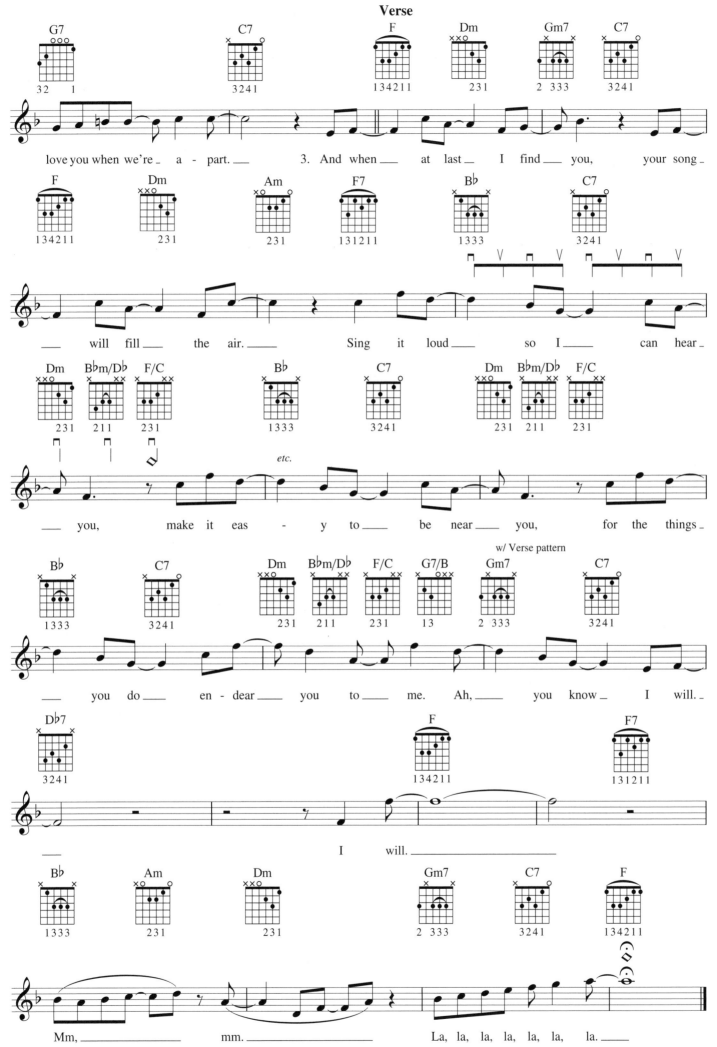

love you when we're a - part. ___ 3. And when ___ at last ___ I find ___ you, your song ___

___ will fill ___ the air. ___ Sing it loud ___ so I ___ can hear ___

etc.

___ you, make it eas - y to ___ be near ___ you, for the things ___

w/ Verse pattern

___ you do ___ en - dear ___ you to ___ me. Ah, ___ you know ___ I will. ___

I will. _____

Mm, _____ mm. ___ La, la, la, la, la, la, la. ___

Let It Be

Words and Music by John Lennon and Paul McCartney

Intro
Slow

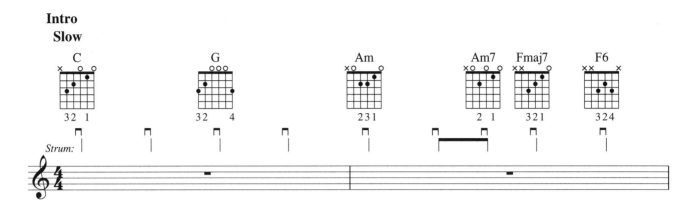

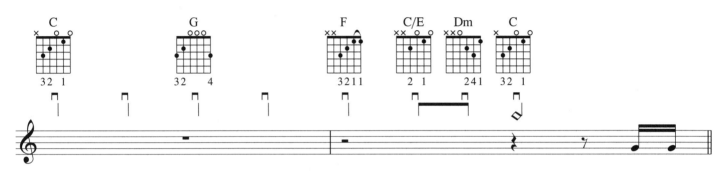

1. When I

𝄋 Verse

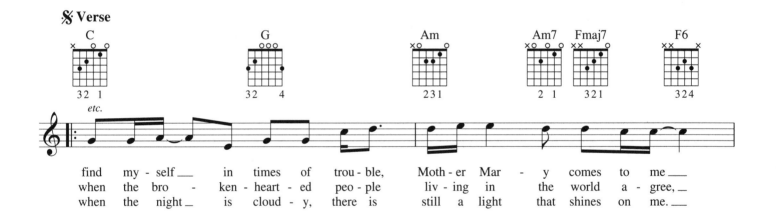

find my-self ___ in times of trou-ble, Moth-er Mar ___ y comes to me ___
when the bro-ken-heart-ed peo-ple liv-ing in the world a-gree, ___
when the night ___ is cloud-y, there is still a light that shines on me. ___

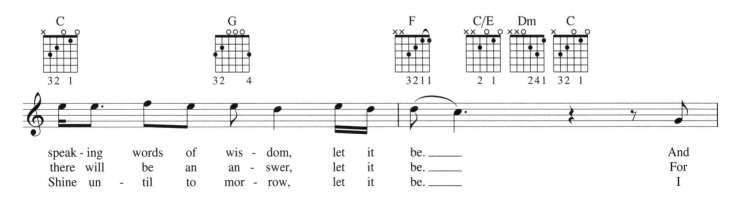

speak-ing words of wis-dom, let it be. ___ And
there will be an an-swer, let it be. ___ For
Shine un-til to mor-row, let it be. ___ I

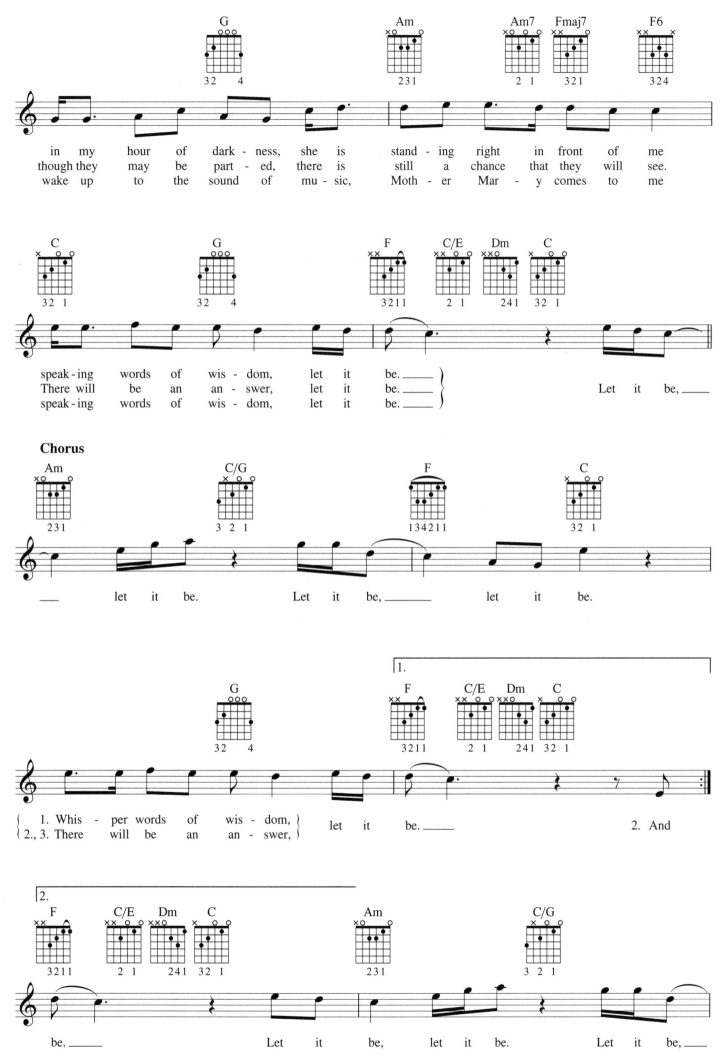

in my hour of dark - ness, she is stand - ing right in front of me
though they may be part - ed, there is still a chance that they will see.
wake up to the sound of mu - sic, Moth - er Mar - y comes to me

speak - ing words of wis - dom, let it be. _____
There will be an an - swer, let it be. _____
speak - ing words of wis - dom, let it be. _____

Let it be, _____

Chorus

_____ let it be. Let it be, _____ let it be.

1.

1. Whis - per words of wis - dom, let it be. _____ 2. And
2., 3. There will be an an - swer,

2.

be. _____ Let it be, let it be. Let it be, _____

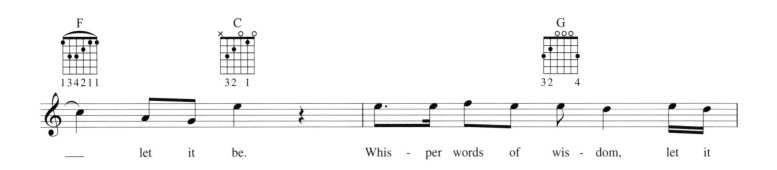

let it be.   Whis - per words of   wis - dom,   let it

Interlude   *To Coda* ⊕

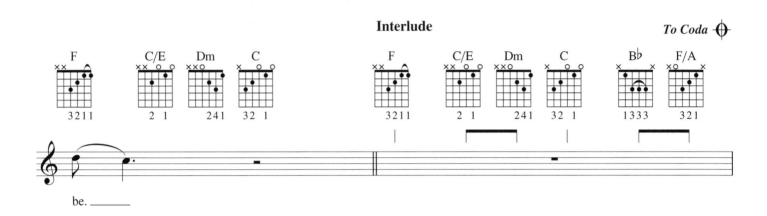

be. _____

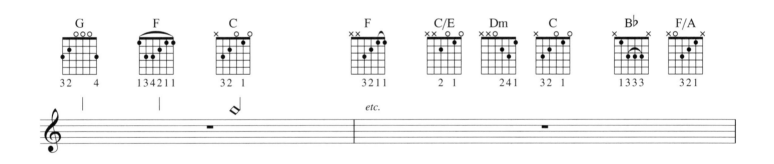

etc.

D.S. al Coda
(take 2nd ending)   ⊕ **Coda**

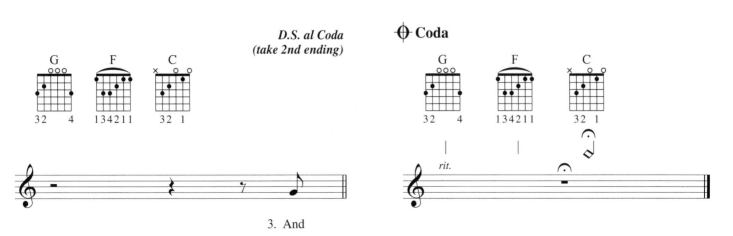

3. And   *rit.*

Ob-La-Di, Ob-La-Da

Words and Music by John Lennon and Paul McCartney

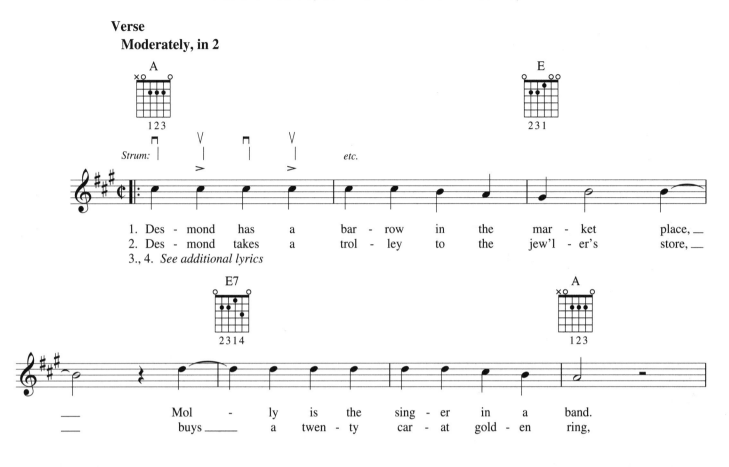

Chorus

___ ob - la - da, _____ life goes on, _____ bra, _____ la, ___

___ la, how their life goes ___ on. _____ Ob - la - di, ___

___ ob - la - da, _____ life goes on, _____ bra, _____

4th time, To Coda ⊕

___ la, _____ la, how their life goes _____ on. _____

1. || 2. **Bridge**

___ In a cou - ple of

years, they have built a home ___ sweet home ___

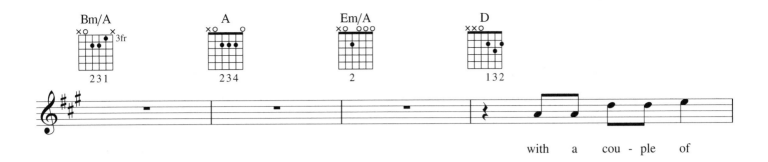

with a cou - ple of

kids run - ning in the yard _____ of

1st time, D.C. (take 2nd ending)
2nd time, D.C. al Coda

Des - mond and Mol - ly Jones. _____

⊕ Coda

And if you want some fun, ___

take ob - la - di - bla - da.

Additional Lyrics

3. Happy ever after in the market place,
   Desmond lets the children lend a hand.
   Molly stays at home and does her pretty face,
   And in the evening she still sings it with the band.

4. Happy ever after in the market place,
   Molly lets the children lend a hand.
   Desmond stays at home and does his pretty face,
   And in the evening she's a singer with the band.

Nowhere Man

Words and Music by John Lennon and Paul McCartney

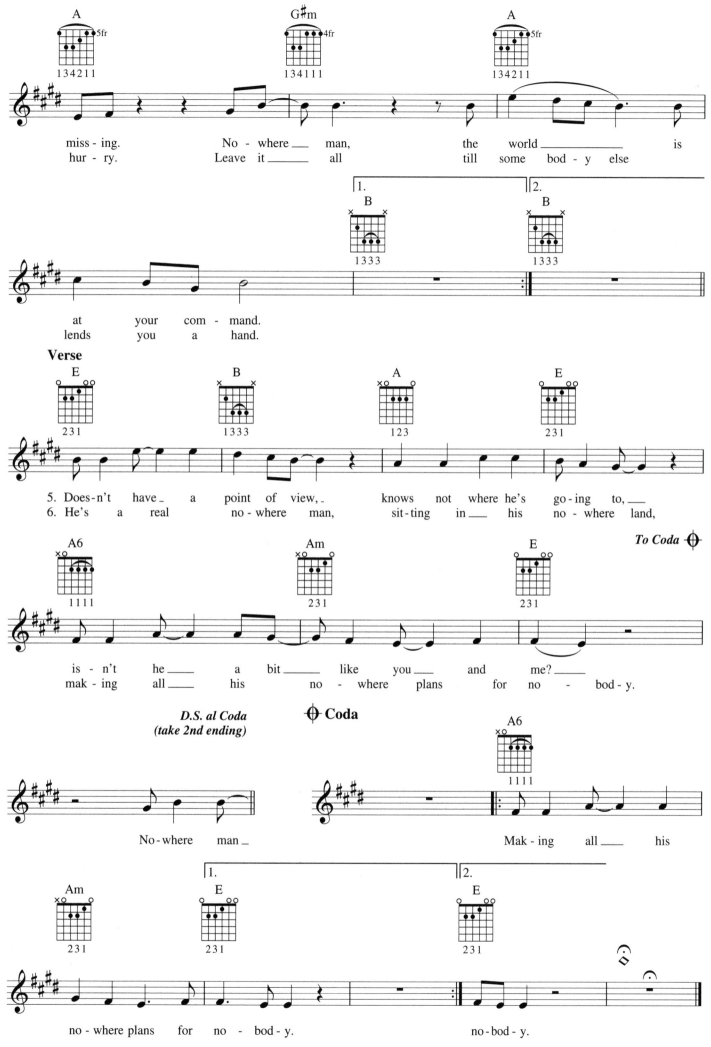

Yellow Submarine

Words and Music by John Lennon and Paul McCartney

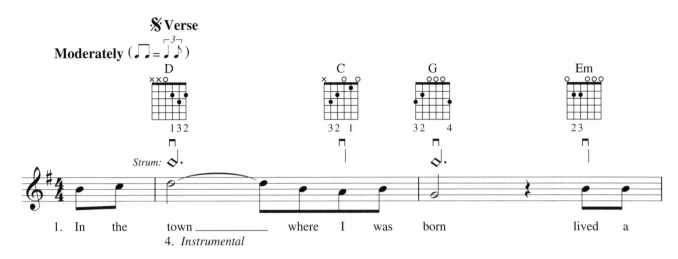

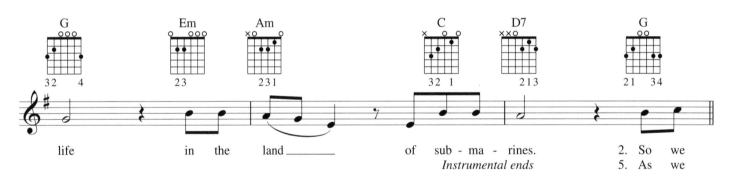

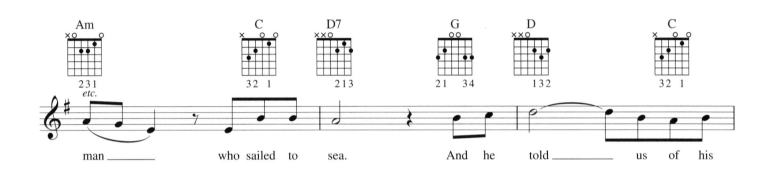

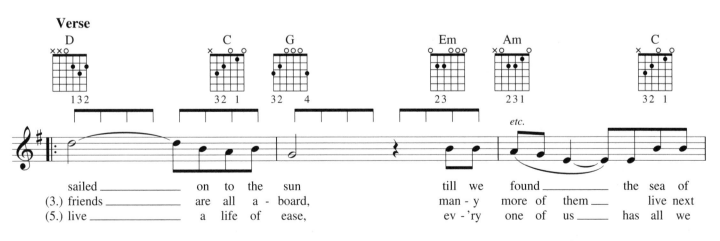

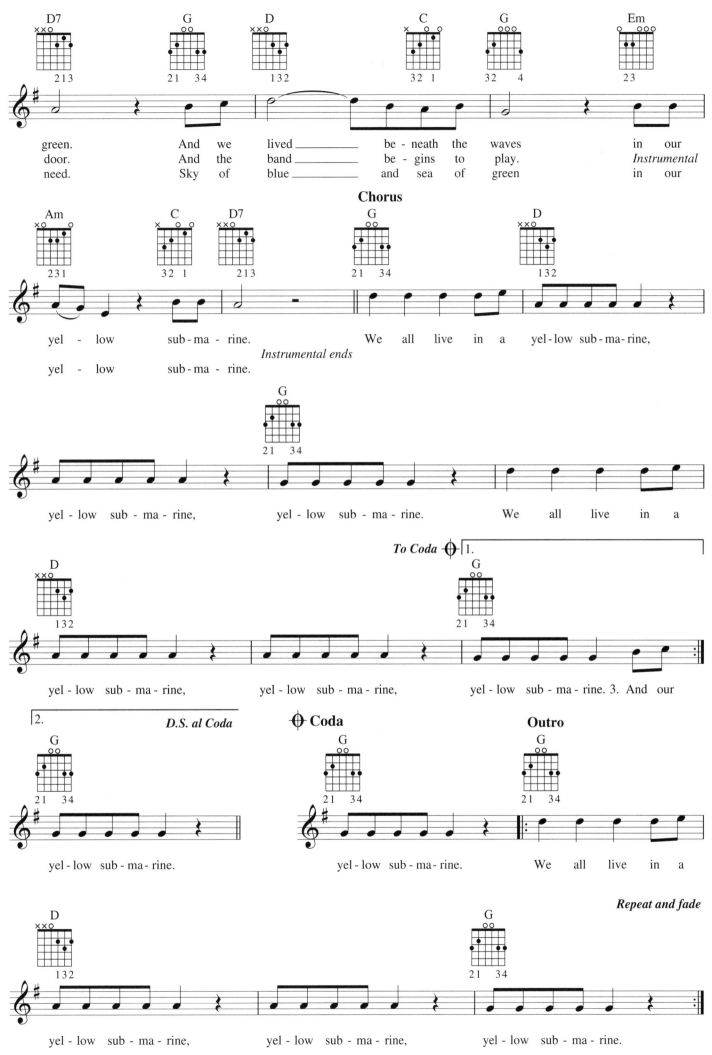

Yesterday

Words and Music by John Lennon and Paul McCartney

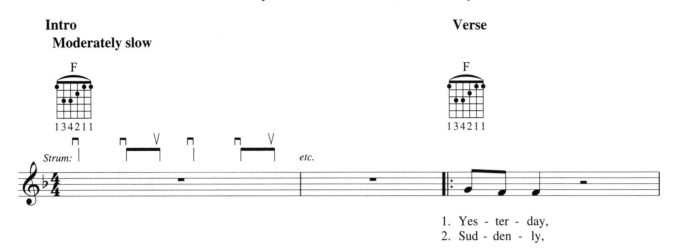

Intro
Moderately slow

Verse

1. Yes - ter - day,
2. Sud - den - ly,

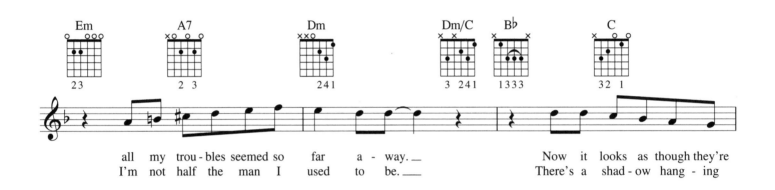

all my trou - bles seemed so   far   a - way. ___   Now it looks as though they're
I'm not half the man I   used   to   be. ___   There's a   shad - ow hang - ing

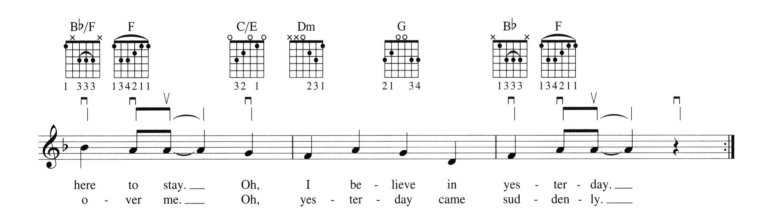

here to stay. ___   Oh,   I   be - lieve   in   yes - ter - day. ___
o - ver me. ___   Oh,   yes - ter - day   came   sud - den - ly. ___

Bridge

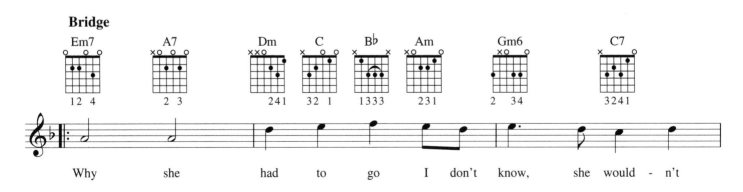

Why   she   had   to   go   I   don't   know,   she would - n't

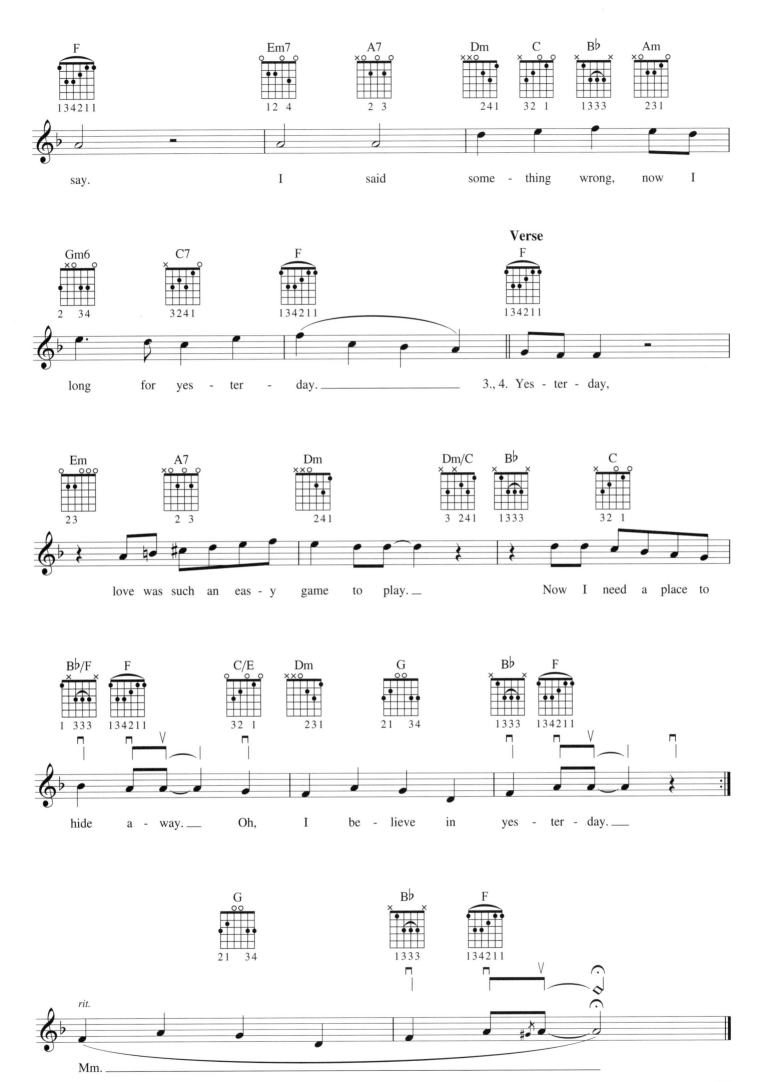

say.   I said some - thing wrong, now I

long for yes - ter - day. _____ 3., 4. Yes - ter - day,

love was such an eas - y game to play. _ Now I need a place to

hide a - way. _ Oh, I be - lieve in yes - ter - day. _

Mm. _____

You've Got to Hide Your Love Away

Words and Music by John Lennon and Paul McCartney

Verse
Slow, in 2

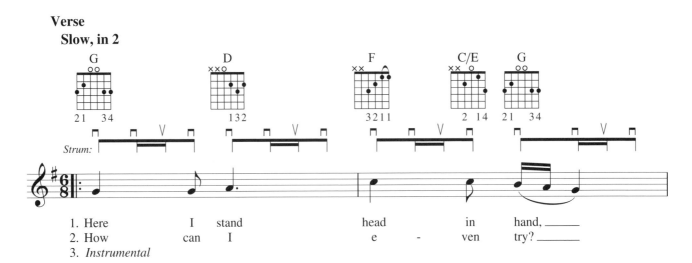

1. Here I stand head in hand,_____
2. How can I e - ven try?_____
3. *Instrumental*

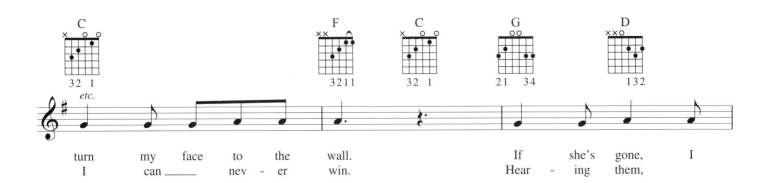

turn my face to the wall.   If she's gone, I
I can_____ nev - er win.   Hear - ing them,

To Coda ⊕

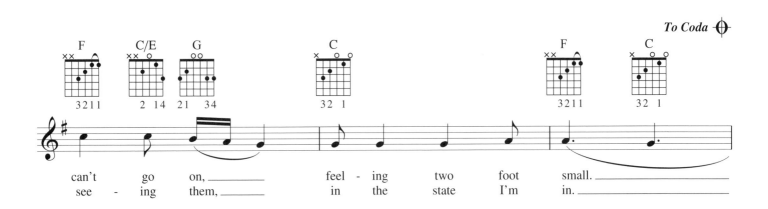

can't go on,_____   feel - ing two foot small._____
see - ing them,_____   in the state I'm in._____

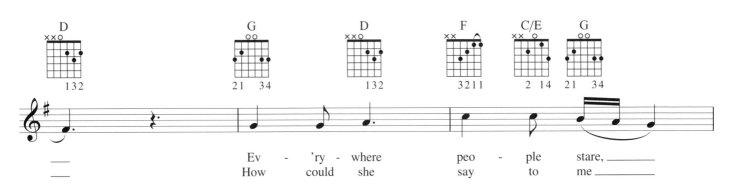

_____   Ev - 'ry - where peo - ple stare,_____
_____   How could she say to me_____

each and ev - 'ry - day.
love will find a way?

I can see them
Gath - er 'round

laugh at me, and I hear them say:
all you clowns, let me hear hear you say:

Chorus

Hey! You've got to

hide your love a - way.

Hey! You've got to hide your love a - way.

2nd time, D.C. al Coda

Coda

Twist and Shout

Words and Music by Bert Russell and Phil Medley

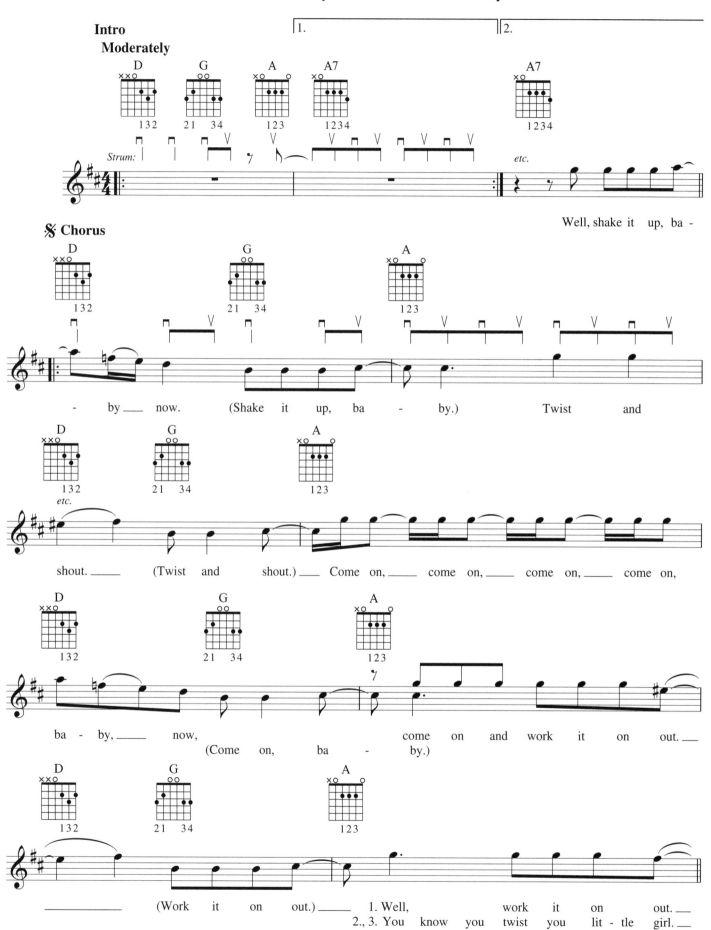

ah,   ah.)   Whoa,   yeah,   yeah! _____ Ba -

⊕ Coda

Chorus

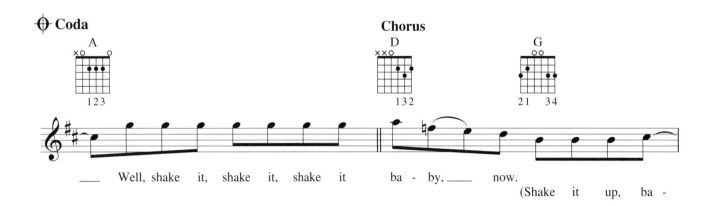

___ Well, shake it, shake it, shake it ba - by, ___ now.
(Shake it up, ba -

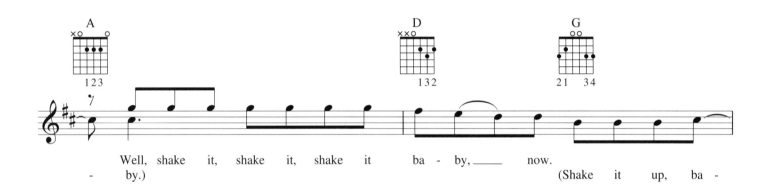

Well, shake it, shake it, shake it ba - by, ___ now.
- by.) (Shake it up, ba -

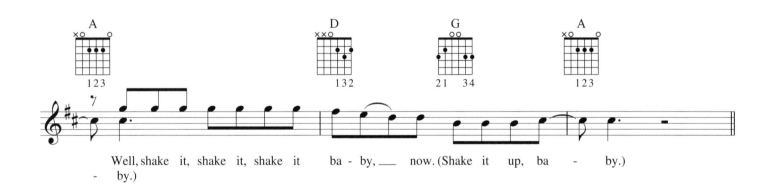

Well, shake it, shake it, shake it ba - by, ___ now. (Shake it up, ba - by.)
- by.)

Outro
w/ Bridge pattern

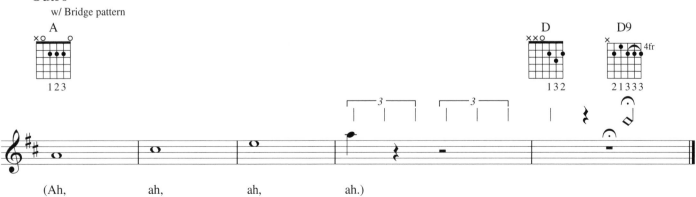

(Ah,   ah,   ah,   ah.)

Guitar Chord Songbooks

Each 6" x 9" book includes complete lyrics, chord symbols, and guitar chord diagrams.

Acoustic Hits
00701787 . . . . $14.99
Acoustic Rock
00699540 . . . . $17.95
Adele
00102761 . . . . $14.99
Alabama
00699914 . . . . $14.95
The Beach Boys
00699566 . . . . $14.95
The Beatles (A-I)
00699558 . . . . $17.99
The Beatles (J-Y)
00699562 . . . . $17.99
Bluegrass
00702585 . . . . $14.99
Blues
00699733 . . . . $12.95
Broadway
00699920 . . . . $14.99
Johnny Cash
00699648 . . . . $17.99
Steven Curtis Chapman
00700702 . . . . $17.99
Children's Songs
00699539 . . . . $16.99
Christmas Carols
00699536 . . . . $12.99
Eric Clapton
00699567 . . . . $15.99
Classic Rock
00699598 . . . . $15.99
Coffeehouse Hits
00703318 . . . . $14.99
Country
00699534 . . . . $14.99
Country Favorites
00700609 . . . . $14.99
Country Standards
00700608 . . . . $12.95
Cowboy Songs
00699636 . . . . $12.95
Creedence Clearwater Revival
00701786 . . . . $12.99
Crosby, Stills & Nash
00701609 . . . . $12.99
John Denver
02501697 . . . . $14.99
Neil Diamond
00700606 . . . . $14.99

Disney
00701071 . . . . $14.99
The Doors
00699888 . . . . $15.99
The Best of Bob Dylan
14037617 . . . . $17.99
Early Rock
00699916 . . . . $14.99
Folksongs
00699541 . . . . $12.95
Folk Pop Rock
00699651 . . . . $14.95
40 Easy Strumming Songs
00115972 . . . . $14.99
Four Chord Songs
00701611 . . . . $12.99
Glee
00702501 . . . . $14.99
Gospel Hymns
00700463 . . . . $14.99
Grand Ole Opry®
00699885 . . . . $16.95
Green Day
00103074 . . . . $12.99
Guitar Chord Songbook White Pages
00702609 . . . . $29.99
Hillsong United
00700222 . . . . $12.95
Irish Songs
00701044 . . . . $14.99
Billy Joel
00699632 . . . . $15.99
Elton John
00699732 . . . . $15.99
Latin Songs
00700973 . . . . $14.99
Love Songs
00701043 . . . . $14.99
Bob Marley
00701704 . . . . $12.99
Paul McCartney
00385035 . . . . $16.95

Steve Miller
00701146 . . . . $12.99
Modern Worship
00701801 . . . . $16.99
Motown
00699734 . . . . $16.95
The 1950s
00699922 . . . . $14.99
The 1980s
00700551 . . . . $16.99
Nirvana
00699762 . . . . $16.99
Roy Orbison
00699752 . . . . $12.95
Peter, Paul & Mary
00103013 . . . . $12.99
Tom Petty
00699883 . . . . $15.99
Pop/Rock
00699538 . . . . $14.95
Praise & Worship
00699634 . . . . $14.99
Elvis Presley
00699633 . . . . $14.95
Queen
00702395 . . . . $12.99
Red Hot Chili Peppers
00699710 . . . . $16.95
Rock Ballads
00701034 . . . . $14.99
Rock 'n' Roll
00699535 . . . . $14.95
Bob Seger
00701147 . . . . $12.99
Sting
00699921 . . . . $14.99
Taylor Swift
00701799 . . . . $15.99
Three Chord Songs
00699720 . . . . $12.95
Top 100 Hymns Guitar Songbook
75718017 . . . . $12.99
Ultimate-Guitar
00702617 . . . . $24.99
Wedding Songs
00701005 . . . . $14.99
Hank Williams
00700607 . . . . $14.99
Neil Young–Decade
00700464 . . . . $14.99

HAL•LEONARD® CORPORATION
7777 W. BLUEMOUND RD. P.O. BOX 13819 MILWAUKEE, WI 53213
Visit Hal Leonard online at **www.halleonard.com**

0813

HAL LEONARD GUITAR CHEAT SHEETS

The Hal Leonard Cheat Sheets series includes lyrics, chord frames, and "rhythm tab" (cut-to-the-chase notation) to make playing easier than ever! No music reading is required, and all the songs are presented on two-page spreads to avoid page turns.

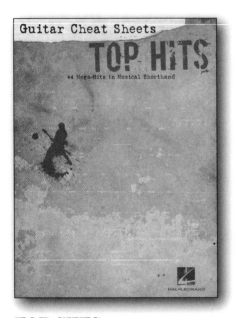

TOP HITS

44 pop favorites, including: Are You Gonna Be My Girl • Baby • Bad Day • Bubbly • Clocks • Crazy • Fireflies • Gives You Hell • Hey, Soul Sister • How to Save a Life • I Gotta Feeling Just the Way You Are • Lucky • Mercy • Mr. Brightside • Need You Now • Take Me Out • Toes • Use Somebody • Viva La Vida • You Belong with Me • and more.
00701646 ....$14.99

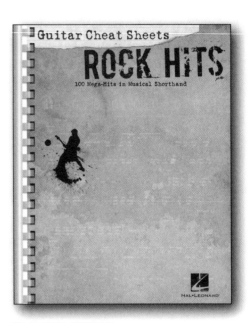

ROCK HITS

44 songs, including: Are You Gonna Go My Way • Black Hole Sun • Counting Blue Cars • Float On • Friday I'm in Love • Gives You Hell • Grenade • Jeremy • Kryptonite • Push • Scar Tissue • Semi-Charmed Life • Smells like Teen Spirit • Smooth • Thnks Fr Th Mmrs • Two Princes • Use Somebody • Viva La Vida • Where Is the Love • You Oughta Know • and more.
00702392 ....$24.99

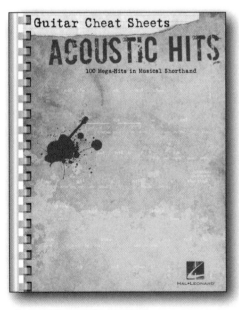

ACOUSTIC HITS

100 unplugged megahits in musical shorthand: All Apologies • Crazy Little Thing Called Love • Creep • Daughter • Every Rose Has Its Thorn • Hallelujah • I'm Yours • The Lazy Song • Little Lion Man • Love Story • More Than Words • Patience • Strong Enough • 21 Guns • Wanted Dead or Alive • Wonderwall • and more.
00702391 ....$24.99

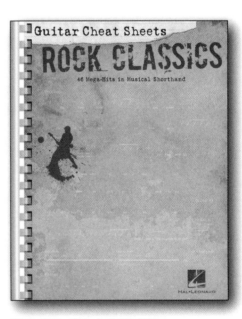

ROCK CLASSICS

Nearly 50 classics, including: All Right Now • Barracuda • Born to Be Wild • Carry on Wayward Son • Cat Scratch Fever • Free Ride • Layla • Message in a Bottle • Paranoid • Proud Mary • Rhiannon • Rock and Roll All Nite • Slow Ride • Smoke on the Water • Sweet Home Alabama • Welcome to the Jungle • You Shook Me All Night Long • and more.
00702393 ....$24.99

HAL•LEONARD® CORPORATION
7777 W. BLUEMOUND RD. P.O. BOX 13819 MILWAUKEE, WI 53213